dogs barking in the distance

John Blackhawk

dogs barking in the distance

Thanks

I would like to thank Liz Macnamara and the other poets of the Friday Night Poets group, who meet every month at The Clearing in Umina Beach, Central Coast, NSW, for the stimulus and constructive criticism given over many years. A special mention for Gillian Telford who gave so much time and thought to improving these poems.

This book is dedicated to my dog, Gracie Groodle, who taught me about loyalty and unconditional love. Forever in your debt. RIP lovely girl.

dogs barking in the distance
ISBN 978 1 76041 784 0
Copyright © text John Blackhawk 2019
Cover photographs: John Blackhawk

First published 2019 by
Ginninderra Press
PO Box 3461 Port Adelaide 5015 Australia
www.ginninderrapress.com.au

Contents

Whale	9
Refuge	10
Poem For an Unknown	12
Only a Dog	14
Some Wild Internal Disorder	16
Desiccated	17
Done Walking	19
Bambusa	20
Is Sweet	22
Poem to Unknown Stargazers	24
Other	26
What's Going On	28
Roppongi	30
Stardog	32
Boat From Kanchanaburi	34
Knock Knock	36
Stuck in Traffic	39
So Much More Besides	41
Phantom	43
Kid Kobane	44
Strange Random	46
Seasoning	48
The Next Ten	49
Koh Chang Vision	51
The Glass and the Breath	53
Komorebi	55
Six Sequential Journeys	56
Ode to the Divine Ms Amphlett	58
Fear of the Day	59
Bullet	60
Poem For Eighteen Lost Women	61

The Poet Goes To War	63
Ningiwi	65
Cullens Road Ghost	67
Bridge Crossing	68
Daughter of Isfahan	69
I Tamas	70
Bewilderness	72
Green Bikini	73
Escape Act	75
High Time	77
I Love You Afghans…	78
Pluviophile	80
OK Commuter	81
Gerald's Shout	83
Jungle	85
Granite	87
Mango	89
University of Pluto Inner Solar System Field Trip…	90
Let Himself Go	92
Nemophilist	93
Anjing	95
Good God	97
Ogre	98
Strangely Strange But Oddly Normal	99
Five Patonga Haiku	103
Trust	104
Fifty Years	106
Enter Stage Left	108
Snakes and Ladders	109
The Lamentation of Bobby the Airedale	110
The Fridge Magnet Poems	112
Shipwreck	113
The Previous Panic of Robert Stamford	114

'Confused Yelling, Muffled Moaning,
Dogs Barking in the Distance'
– from the hearing-impaired subtitles to the film
Enemy At the Gates

'Poets are those with the courage to leave ajar the door to
madness.' – Christopher Morley

Whale

you turned up off Pearl Beach uninvited
one of our distant relatives

we believe we lord it over you
because we have digital clocks timeshare apartments food colourings
and I suppose I could mention here
armed conflict political factions greenhouse emissions
but suddenly I find my sunnyday-upmood plummeting

some say it was a mistake we came down from the trees
I'm sure you're pleased your lot kept going clear to the coast

from here you can see Lion Pitt Palm and Whale
an island named for a wild cat
a stretch of water named for a dead politician
a beach named after a family of plants
another beach named for you the whole lot of you I guess

do you name your waters reefs and headlands
after fish seaweeds and famous dead cetaceans?
do they sound like clicks whoops and groans?

we're not nice we've got nations
who all want a piece of you

but you're not that innocent
we've seen on television what your orcas can do

still I wish I had a tail that splashed like that
and could hold my breath for hours in the deep deep green alongside you

Refuge

the little English kid ran full tilt along the waterfront

past the spice warehouses and stalls
pungent with pepper saffron and turmeric
which he still couldn't distinguish
flew past the wooden boats
dark skinny men prodding the water at the prow and stern
smell of waterweeds and mauve and yellow lilies
reflections of palms and Kerala's purple hills
turned sharp right round the fruit and vegetable traders
squatting women shouted in Malayalam and laughed at the sight
a sudden whiff of mango on the wheezed in-breath
thumping heart and flailing arms
past the hidden bungalows lining both sides
a mass of post-monsoon growth obscuring the walls
two squirrels scrambled up a banyan tree
bolted past the chipped orange Ganesh statue by the temple
garlands of heat-fatigued flowers dangling around its trunk

he spilled breathless into a park of clipped frangipani and hibiscus
just like the ones at the sprawling bungalow
with the drunk and damaged mother
and the denying and damaged father
the absent sister at boarding school in the Nilgiri hills
the ayah who held to him cold cloths when the fever came
and who sweated spices through her sandalwood skin
and spoke in tones that said she knew his heart

the cook who made kedgeree every day
the gardener who handed over cut papaya on the sly
the friendly dogs who knew every secret place he knew
the occasional visiting cobra panicking the whole household
the frequently visiting monkeys not much better

banking around curved paths in the park
panting like the exhausted elephant in the street last week
sweat running down his suntanned legs into the dusty sandals
there the line of forest and beyond
the slow sliding cool green backwaters of Alleppey
rice boats and small huts and the stoic Keralans

ask for refuge with any of them
ask for nothing more than they offer
ask for a different life

from the one
I've gone back to tell him
is coming his way

Poem For an Unknown

This 35-line poem is dedicated to the wolf in a 35-second Facebook video

I write to you from the warm southern summer
knowing you sit in the snow
in your frigid northern landscape
knowing I do not know you
knowing I never can

so how to tell you my boy
or are you a girl or not even young
that you have reached through everything
and touched me like nothing I remember?
just how can I do anything?

but doing must happen
or I will not rest easy
so this is for you love
you beautiful black wolf
watching the snow fall

flakes nestling in your fur
flakes floating past those eyes
those eyes those soulful eyes
sorrowful eyes knowing eyes
blinking ever so slowly

the upward tilt of your head
happens at glacial speed
exuding serenity and calm
sniffing in the snow flurry
blinking and squeezing your eyes

it took days to decode
the message you sent me
of your acceptance and hope
this is how it is sometimes
the snow falls then it stops

how come after all these years
when I have stubbornly ignored
the pleadings of other humans
an unknown black wolf has told me
everything will be all right?

Only a Dog

for Gracie Groodle, 16 June 2004–31 March 2017, loved, lost and to be forever remembered

clawsteps on the wooden floor
they're just some tippy-tappy ghost
the sound of flopping on the carpet
only someone dropping a bag
that excited bark at the postman
is the mutt up the avenue

I struggle…
…with pronouns
they must become she
them must now be her
…with tenses
changing do to did
and have to had
is to was
…with plurals
that 's' in dogs
is as stubborn as dull pain
…with numbers
two of everything once
now things are in the singular

the only time she broke my heart
was the day she left us
when I go too I want to see her
waiting at the end of that tunnel
holding her lead in her mouth

I reach out...

nothing of her resists my hand

Some Wild Internal Disorder

'…some wild internal disorder beyond medicine remained in his quaking soul.' – Richard Flanagan in *The Narrow Road To the Deep North*

How dark the silence how bright the violence breaking our days!
Waiting in this jungle chasm all hope forsaking the tedious days.

Random bestiality kills all reason here and it's all they have.
Scouring our skin ripping us up and raking our toiling days.

At twilight's edge I still see the dead calling for a last smoke –
the reaching, racked breathing, men never waking to new days.

Strange we remember the girls back home like postcard views –
motionless transfixed and posed for cameras on baking hot days.

We lionhearts covered in rags on scabby skeletons shuffle
into the gloom – entropy making nightmares of our days.

Desiccated

at long last the daily blue
gives way to rolling greys and whites
tumbling and puffy
then overloaded and leaden
the bureau confirms it
it's the real thing
really this time it is

I stand under cover
to marvel at what is commonplace
even annoying to peoples
in other locations
delight that the bird poo
starting to bake on the duco
from yesterday's rude flock of galahs
won't need the carwash
and how many hours will I save
not having to stand under the brassy sky
hose in hand spraying out succour
to a garden on the edge of drought?

yellow verges change to green
at the speed of chameleons
wildflowers bounce out of dry earth
birds bathe like squawky kids
in brown pools by the roadside
no doubt various reptiles
find their own secret drinking spots

I watch it come down hard
from the deck out the back
suddenly the turning wind
showers periwinkle-coloured blossoms
all over the greening lawn
jacarandas and rainstorms
the short desiccating winter washed away

early in the morning
I turn onto my back
lie and listen
to the staccato splatting
on the awning outside the bedroom
the dances for rain have worked
but our dreams are dreamt in the dry
what's this?
smiling at ten past four?

Done Walking

it's all your fault you two shaggy dogs
I'm trawling the ocean line under leaden black clouds
blowing heavy and loaded from Sydney way
through four distinct showers when I could be inside
a man and his dogs on the edge of the world
when I could be washing up
instead done tight up rain dripping from my hood

a dead pelican is revered by you both
another glides around the crash site
like an avian spirit from the birdy hereafter
warragarra the sea eagle makes no error with scale
and thankfully gives us a miss
as the air turns grey as slate all around
the horizon dissolves and I am undone

Bambusa

'Bamboo means all things to some people,
and some things to all people' – ancient Chinese saying

my eyes adjusted to the green shade
and I curled my digit finger and braced it
against my thumb
and tapped

on a windy day in the parklands
detoured into the grove again
to hear it creak like a shogun's warship
running in front of a typhoon

to look up into the cloud-scudding sky
at the jostling wispy leaves
that grow like fresh green pixels on steep hillsides
lunch for browsing giant pandas

to trace the culms and shoots
about fifteen centimetres between nodes
to embrace the smooth stems with my palms
did I say I am prone to tree-hugging anyway?

to hear the spirit of the air
laugh the tubular laughter of green shoots
compose the botanical music of wind chimes
play Zen notes to an audience of one

to be sectioned and formed into flutes
to grieve like refugees
never to return to their soil

stepped out into parkland glare
in this beautiful place overwhelmed

the mournful song of the reed

Is Sweet

the clues were there for weeks
but the young man didn't want to believe
she wouldn't do it would she?
yet still he tracked her car out of town
up the valley road for fifteen minutes
hid while she kissed the man by the door

if you know people and have money
it's easy to get a powerful rifle
pick a date you're certain of
fix yourself a foolproof alibi
no need to rush the thing
a dish best served cold they say

an old man a mile away stood up fast
a gunshot down the valley
dropped the weeding fork
his retriever barking at his side
a scream at the house down there
and a surprised shout straight after

didn't take the detectives long
dead man shot from up a tree
shooter falls out of said tree
probably underestimating recoil
breaks neck and dies instantly
crime of passion so it seemed

Confucius had it right
but even he would be surprised
how it can sometimes play out
before you embark
on a journey of revenge
dig two graves

Poem to Unknown Stargazers

staring at southern stars at three-thirty
sleepless and thoughtful
a sleep that burned like yours

perhaps it's around midnight or just pre-dawn
when your anxiety got you up
like me a restless stargazer

in New Caledonia a village
where fishing boats leave before sunrise
a twenty-year-old fisherman night-smoking

in New Guinea on the banks of the Sepik
fretting about the hunt tomorrow
a troubled tribal chief in waiting

in the South Island near Haas
you walk out from your home in the hills
planning a huge Maori funeral

in the Pilbara flat out on the sand
you can see Old Man Emu up there
but you're worrying about your baby's cough

way up the coast on the luminescent Coral Sea
a vodka and lime on the deck
you or the boat one of you has to go

we're all six of us out here in the night pleading
to gods and deities imagined old and modern
for a better day than yesterday turned out
a day that unravelled our plans too fast
set us on a course we never asked for
broke dreams years in the making
got us staring and hoping to god
there is a divine presence

Other

Inspired by the sorrows from John Koenig's *Dictionary of Obscure Sorrows*

sideways glimpses as I race by an arcade
there can you see?
there he goes
his life more coloured more vibrant in most aspects
he owns yachts and fast cars
basks in tropical pools cocktail in hand
sleeps in a bedroom with bamboo creaking outside
through the open door and beyond
there can you hear it?
the lap-lap of a warm ocean under an ochre moon
and do I feel I am him?
a him that could have existed?
I get a subtle peripheral feeling
when I'm falling asleep sometimes
that he is me at least
but mostly when awake I wish to care less
loosen my grip on this life I have
to not care about the sneak thief stalking me
after my wallet phone keys and photos
because these things are left in some locked vault
I long ago lost the key for
then it turns out that standing in a forest
darkness hanging green
walking on a beach in the rain
waves crashing and splashing negative ions around
that a peak feeling pervades my moments
but then squeezing through an ever-widening chink
hypothetical conversations covering every occasion

arguments with aspects of me
criticisms of behaviour current and past
coherent arguments no part of me can discount
with subpersonalities who annoy irritate and obstruct my world
and I know that the feeling of being on top
will dissipate like dust in a gale
that immediately on becoming happy
inevitably I will start on the downward spiral
of murmuring about politics money tax phone calls
and the knowledge I've been trapped in professions too long
and I always get disturbed that I cannot know
how our history will pan out
exactly where and how we will fall into the abyss
the timing of our Armageddon
who will be last one standing?
the expansiveness felt at high times is lost
when I hear the thumping of a massive thunderstorm
and I get cocooned in the familiar enclosure of my room
awash in an amniotic tranquillity

What's Going On

my tombstone?
given up on *rust in peace*
because the pin in my ankle is the offspring
of space shuttle and tennis racquet technology
and has a half-life of six million years
and is hardly qualified to represent me
given up on *he was a good bloke*
not inviting corrections to that one by my graveside
given up too on *he would like to thank all the singer dancer artist*
vegetarian girls and women whose arms he strayed into
though there had been this pattern
also given up on *he helped over 38,000 migrant and refugee kids*
settle and grow more prosperous than he ever was
though it's a fact of my life
he taught maths too
invites graffiti good riddance stuff you and pythagoras
and i've given up on the number thing you know the sort
he consumed 258 chickens 8.6 tonnes of potatoes 1,767 corn cobs
1309 bottles of chardonnay and 4 large shoals of fish
because i just don't have the stats
the same reason i've given up on
he waited 6 years 25 weeks 1 day 16 hours and 27 minutes
for various girlfriends and wives to try on clothes shoes hats handbags
though i reckon i'm closer on this score
and it was probably the cause of death
i have given up on my mobile number
and a website

where you can view my photo gallery download my favourite tracks
but not given up yet on
hopefully
@heaven
.com.au

Roppongi

sat in a small park late evening
a huge metallic spider sculpture above me
its coloured lights sweeping into shadowy bushes
and across the bench where I sat
and where another coughing fit has me gasping

prepare by hyperventilating
make sure my spine is straight
cough and wheeze
cough and wheeze
hope not to vomit
pray not to black out

sat with aching neck muscles
and popped red eyes
recovering in a neon-lit food palace
tempura and miso

then the I'm-all right-we-can-walk
and the long stroll along urban streets
past red light glinting Tokyo Tower
under bridges with *densha* gliding on rails above
carrying late commuters and shoppers
a night *shinkansen* heading for Kyoto and Nara

stopping at every vending machine
the blessed medicine for my week in Japan
glorious sweet Royal Tea sipped all the way
to my bed in Toranamon

and another night of coughing bouts
sitting on the end of the bed
in the gaps staring through the window
at the galaxy of red glinting lights
thinking should I dress and go out to Shibuya
wander the music stores
or give myself a chance of an hour's dreaming again
the cemeteries in the bamboo forests in Kamakura
the temples in the tangled gardens
or the castle in Ueno with its thick wedge shaped walls
probably the graphite spider in Roppongi too

in Japan I walked and walked
through my whooping cough days
tried out my nipon-go on everyone I could
but it was often wrong and not much more than
hello goodbye please thank you yes no
made the most of it
hyperventilate straighten hope pray

Stardog

observing him jogging beside
He's getting old.
I don't count the years.
I don't multiply by seven.

under scudding dark clouds
skirting the shoreline
in a gale of stinging rain
man and dog together

such a bond with this alien
who would follow me
without any canine indecision
to the ends of the earth

he never questions his fidelity
given without condition
a permanent best friend is what you get
not some human fair-weather one

loyalty functioning like therapy
after that dished out by people
a Nobel prize lies in wait for the person
who can coax fifty years from a dog

They bred dogs for everything else
even diving for fish
why didn't they breed them to live longer
to live as long as a man?

homo sapiens and *canis domesticus*
personal contact with an extra terrestrial
happy fellow beachcomber
little brother my heart

quotes in italics from *The Dog Stars* by Peter Heller (published by Headline Press)

Boat From Kanchanaburi

Pataporn calls me to eat
pad thai and prawns
like nearly every day
smell it steaming
in our bamboo bowls
and I'm so hungry now

carved another little boat yesterday
all evening by the kerosene light
after eighteen years
it still takes over four hours
the seats and prow take longest
as if I don't have enough of boats

was a poor catch today
hardly worth a hundred baht
won't pay for Wacharee's tablets
hold the wooden boat up
one of my best efforts
and all the paddles made

later will carve the elephants
then curl up with Patti
in the stifling Kanchanaburi night
get it to the shop tomorrow
make up for the lack of fish
get the medicine for Wachi

elephants paddling a boat!
love rustic artisan carvings!
from Thailand you say?
yep from Kanchanaburi…

and not a day goes past
without me smiling at it

Knock Knock

what's the use of these poets?
we'll be at war with Boney soon
what's one of them going to do?
kill a Froggy archer with a sonnet?

bailiffs like me will be called
honest working men will fight
we'll leave without protest
when his like will run and hide

he owns a house in Nether Stowey
owes the king for window and land tax
money we need for the coming war
and I'm the man to collect it

Georgie may be a lunatic
but he's regent of our England
and we all pay him his due
except wastrels like these poets

been after this one for months
a wild goose chase every time
when I enter a village inn
he was always there yesterday

then today good fortune smiles
find he's repaired to Ash Farm
Robert Crowcombe's place
near enough to my Porlock home

even on this inclement autumn day
I'm walking like a spring chicken
up the rambling muddy path
past half a dozen doleful horses

can't be much to this poetry lark
easier than balancing figures
keeping abreast of court business
might write a poem myself later on

Mary Crowcombe lets me in
offers me lunch and an ale
got no mind for that at all
Show me to his room!

knock on the heavy door
must be three inches of oak
not a sound comes from inside
hit it again and bruise my hand

Confound it! Who's that?
Nathaniel Greenwood tax collector.
I'm occupied with writing man.
Open the door Mister Coleridge…

In October 1797, the poet, Samuel Taylor Coleridge, was walking from Lynton on the north Devon coast to his home at Nether Stowey in Somerset. He became sick and retired to a farmhouse near Porlock.

Opium was prescribed, which caused him to fall asleep in his chair. During this sleep, he said he had composed two or three hundred lines of an epic poem he was going to call 'Kubla Khan'. On waking, he eagerly wrote down the first few dozen lines. Then he answered the door to a petty official who detained him for an hour over some taxation matter.

Coleridge was unable to remember any more of his poem. 'All the rest had passed away like the images on the surface of a stream into which a stone had been cast.'

Stuck in Traffic

peripheral vision is picking out
to one side a hill covered in ironbarks
cockatoos flapping through the canopy
to the other a silver waterway
diamonds covering the rippling surface
but right in my sights in front of me
another car come to a halt
like mine and the one behind
a snake of vehicles tracing the curve
the screech of three kinds of sirens
two ambulances a police car and a fire engine
some poor buggers are not going home
usually this sobers me up and I feel grateful
to have more days and not be them
today I feel deeprootedly blue
dismayed despondent disillusioned
and the idiot in front has his foot on the brake
the red glare adding to my mood
turn off my ignition turn to the side
the glittering water sparkles
a line of marching clouds on the horizon
and my blueness deepens to a chasm
they call it black dog
the black dogs in my home
always look pretty happy to me
out of the corner of my eyes the brake lights
both ambulances wail past
car drivers are out and peering forward
chatting in that banal way they do
in the presence of injury

Schadenfreude I suppose
better text my wife
don't feel like talking
back late stuck in traffic
is all it needs to be
hate the predictive text
back late stuck in tragic
send it anyway
mouth curling
is that the beginning
of a smile?

So Much More Besides

for Nick Drake, singer-songwriter born Yangon, Burma, 1948, died
Tanworth-in-Arden, Warwickshire, England, 1977

through your attic window
you had an unrestricted view
across Warwickshire fields
in hazy autumnal mists
horse chestnut dropping crimson
wan sunsets hanging lightly
soft dustings of snow
the spire of the village church
like taunting to you
aspire or die

from outside your window
anyone who cared to would see
the messy book-strewn desk
the notepads of scratched lyrics
the two guitars and spare strings
a teapot on the bedside table
bottle of pills in an open drawer
they would witness you
composing rare work in this space
while you decomposed slowly inside

the window a telescope and a microscope
you saw too much without
far far too much within
and so much more besides
till your day was done
if you had known you had a brother like me
that you brightened his northern sky
we would both have been saved from blue
because time has told me
connection is thicker than blood

Phantom

again a beautiful desolation
drops like a heavy cloak
something solid breaks inside

i remember moments spent with you

always the same triggers
a neon-lit night
bass and sax on the car radio
glow of the car dials in the dash
water trickling on the windscreen
traffic lights switching green to red
reflecting in rain pools

the swirling close-up memories
your eyelashes brush my cheek
your hair like strands of crystal
that perfume and those vivid lips
you whisper implying seduction
gorgeous phantom from my past
circling the edge of consciousness

soul mate who once brushed my life

not this night but one coming
you will step back from me
make yourself known

Kid Kobane

uncle Aziz came back up north
with an English-made ludo game
from one of the souks in Damascus
we boys always grabbed the red and green
the colours of our country's flag
leaving our sisters to the blue and yellow

we played through freezing Kobane evenings
on the table with its overhead gaslight
and in long hot school summer holidays
under the plastic sheeting in the courtyard
four colours in deadly competition
no chores for the winner that day

now my wife and our two are walking
walking somewhere with uncle Aziz
and my two sisters and their kids
maybe through Turkey Greece Hungary Serbia
who knows how they are or even if they are
two months and nothing comes back this way

they call me Kid Kobane here in Al Raqqah
where I wait behind a smashed stone wall
a captured semi-automatic in my hands
dust in my eyes and in my water bottle
Farid beside me talks loudly smokes carelessly
not for the first time either

in this catastrophic crucible
it's Al Assad Al Nusra ISIL and the Kurds
four colours of evil in deadly combat

Syrian and Turkish planes up there
and now the Russians and Yanks fly over too
threatening to tip up the board

Farid thinks it's all a bit of fun
thinks he'll come out alive!

hey Farid you ever play ludo?

Strange Random

the grevillea out the front dies suddenly
black stems and powdering leaves

the woman has impossibly blue eyes
no one can avoid these jewels

the forms of bacteria under the scope
look like they should be hung on a wall

the sweep of almost orange sand
curving into a vanishing point

the spotted quoll sipping the creek
near the waterfall early morning

cancer cells virile and vivacious
are gorgeous when you don't know

the black dog turned upside down
waiting for a belly scratch

the five petalled frangipani flowers
exuding a scent that causes swooning

the languid groper fish gleaming blue
drifts past the porthole of your mask

the soughing in she-oaks
from a slow hot wind

teriyaki and tempura like sculpture
on a black plate with cherry blossoms

the huge provincial afghan rug
a woven work lighting up the room

beauty is well distributed

Seasoning

it comes pouring from the troposphere
battering on the metal roof of the patio
in the midst of power-cutting storms
that dazzle like exploding stars in the night
bellow as though sky gods are dying
comes washing plants from their containers
pouring over inadequate guttering
relieving the sauna-like conditions
which give me prescient headaches
more reliable than the bureau of met

next morning you walk outside
gaze up at the clearest blue light
lorikeets trill in the eucalypts nearby
splashes of primaries from a mad painter

that morning you sip your coffee
look down at the bright green grass
now obliterated by jacaranda petals
denoting this season of purple rain

The Next Ten

been about two thousand years now
you've been counting from zero
since the year of His birth
by the way you got that wrong
you were four years too early
and He wasn't a Capricorn
gave you plenty of clues about fishes
hardly any about goats

you didn't do well with the last ten
so here's an updated set of rules
for your next two millennia
probably your last chance at it
might pull the plug around 4000
giving up on the thou shalt not…
probably misjudged you there
need to be more imperative now

coveting your neighbour's ox
needs a serious update agreed
but the bit about killing must stay
all this murder war and terrorism
you have a working majority in hell now
never expected I'd be saying that
don't have this trouble on other worlds
oh and stop killing yourselves too

so stop killing each other
stop taunting my bears
stop hunting my whales
stop wrecking the rainforests
where my orangutans live
in fact treat all my animals
like you would each other
actually much better than that

stop polluting my oceans
stop dirtying my air
stop ripping down my forests
stop rushing around
stop eating so much
if you humans get it wrong again
you'll be switched off
your world will go to the dogs

Koh Chang Vision

in the water on the west coast of Koh Chang
the sky is saturated
drips like a trillion waterfalls
into a pearlised sea
a warm bath of a sea
lapping around my suntanned knees
plastic clogs sucking into the seaweedy sand
too bloody hot
so gaspingly bloody hot
coconut palms lean out
over the Gulf of Thailand
I tie my shirt round my neck
fend off the hazy sunshine
the straw hat drooping over my eyes
the stone pendant stuck to my breastbone

I wade along with visions of refugees in the dark
silently stealing towards boats bound for the horizon
visions of allied soldiers shouldering their Lee-Enfields
stealthily moving around Jap positions
Khmer Rouge gun runners carrying boxes in pairs
threatening locals with curved hunting knives
and all this intruding on my tropical holiday
like a death at a birthday party

then the coconut
the blessed coconut
drifted into my shin
hermetically and botanically sealed
its cargo of germinating potential safe in the husk
a wanderer as am I
its destination unpredictable
its past a mystery
from here? from Koh Khlum? another country?
somewhere across this glassy sea
a meanderer condemned and privileged to drift
floating with currents and tides
in the attempt at getting a beachhead on land
to burst into life to grow bud flower
and bear fruit

stooping I pick the coconut out of the salt
run my hands around its green skin
feel its warts and scars
hold it to my heart
take it in
see it is all about the future
not someone else's past
not even mine

The Glass and the Breath

focus that lens
blow on those sparks

fine kindling gathered in a pile
magnifying glass and the breath of El Niño
and we ants must hurtle for our lives

myriad of warm colours
startling gamut of forms
my garden has turned into a thing of wonder

plants purchased and propagated
cuttings from wherever I could
plants rescued from roadsides

looked after daily before I was
derailing most of my life
caused me to even miss holidays

committed to vigilant observation
shifted plants around for the best
found optimum positions for life

patrolled for slugs and mealy grubs
killed aphids and scale
looked after plants when sickness struck
dedicated trips to buy seaweed tonics
fertiliser and mulch
the best organic compost
no let up for more than six years
though a few got lost

watched the weather
predicted and prepared
let's count the hours watering
standing in the brassy sun
encouraging melanomas
let's see 6 times 52 times 7
would give us an hour a day
my garden knows it's more

photosynthesis going on behind my back
and in broad daylight
shooting and sprouting stems twigs and branches
laying down lignin
all the time producing fuel
manufacturing botanical incendiaries
setting down a thatch of leaves and bark
a groundswell of fire starters

surrounded by the fuel dump of bushland beyond
one hot day it will lay fiery siege to my home
now the enemy grows large within the gates

I stand breathless in this heatwave
awaiting the glass and the breath

Komorebi*

smell of damp leaves on the path
dry sclerophyll after the showers
angophora turpentine and ironbark trees
grey boulders mossy on the south side

sun dropped over the mountain
red beams came piercing through
dots stars and sparkles danced
turned the Sydney red gums crimson

it flapped its wings around me
and a hurricane whipped up inside
butterfly effect in my core
brief transforming moment

heavenly light will filter through
when no one is around as witness
someone up there made a mistake
for all of twenty seconds

* komorebi – the sunlight that filters through trees (Japanese)

Six Sequential Journeys

we thundered in from the east lands
and we are going to stay here now
stegosaurs and therapods are easy meat
sheltering in their dark cycad forests
crocodiles and sharks to kill in the mangroves
they will call us *Megalosaurus broomensis*

we went walkabout in the dry season
from the cape right down to the peninsula
where the salt marshes sting our cracked feet
along the mangroves watching out for crocodiles
we the Yawuru people of the coastal flats
have been coming here since The Dreaming

we sailed The Roebuck around the red rocky point
natives kept their distance when we went ashore
otherworldly plants I drew so many in that bay
I Captain William Dampier of Somerset England
will have this mangrove-filled bay named for my ship
will have the peninsula named for me by God I will

we rowed ashore five months ago eleven pearl men
Orang Mutiara from the coast of west Sumatra
diving a gasping dive deep onto the oyster beds all day
handing over the treasure to the Orang Australia
who will drink themselves to violence in their alehouses
but our pearls will adorn the necks of beauties in Sydney

we streaked in low across Cable Beach on the third day of March 1942
me in command of nine Dai 3 Kotukai Mitsubishi A6M2 Zero fighters
strafed the Aussie and Yankee planes at the tiny airport there
smashed the sea planes and ships in Roebuck Bay killing the refugees
the Imperial Japanese Navy Air Service will have a medal for me
they will sing songs in sake houses about Lieutenant Zenjiro Miyano

we flew into the airport from Perth above salt marshes and sand flats
then on approach the sudden glory of Cable Beach and Roebuck Bay
alighting with new friends from Canada and Germany
from the backpackers' hostel we will visit a pearl farm
drink mango beer at Matsos Japanese brewery
in two more weeks we can tick Broome off our bucket lists

Ode to the Divine Ms Amphlett

blundering into the hotel on the northern beaches
heavily drunk full of laughs and lunacy
a cavernous warehouse stinking of beer and ciggies
summer of 83 higher than clouds

even through the alcohol fog i knew
i was in one of those rare wrenching moments
smacked in the gob like in a pub brawl
time has changed colour and moved off somewhere

darkness and shouting spotlights and sound
you were standing barely three metres away
your mike a light sabre swirling
and we were all your boys in town

you a wild dervish woman
all fringe eyeliner and pouting lips
a school uniform stockings a flash of thigh
daring us all to not want you right there

the challenge and threat in your voice
a banshee and angel all at once
when you sang hey little boy
you meant us and we felt so small

chrissy i never felt pleasure like that night
got lost searching for you in other women

Fear of the Day

budgie smugglers and topless girls
backyard cricket at the holiday home up the coast
smell of citronella on the deck all evening
short southerly buster and the search for a jumper
back then a summer you could trust

standing on the lookout at dawn
red sky in the morning
is everyone's warning
our new found fear of the day
and the burning and burning and bushfires stinking

damaging winds up from the south
gusting wildly smashing gardens panicking dogs
rain cascading from concrete coloured skies
rotting the native plants cacti and succulents
and the pouring and pouring and rivers bursting

found a woman's knickers at the lookout
a black lacy symbol of man's careless thrusting
mother earth gets screwed just like this

Bullet

dodged one last week

surrounded by the gowned ones
efficient in their business
matter of fact their routine
bleeping machines
and that spotless smell
reminders of past broken bones

electrodes on my chest
the probing for veins
then like a prisoner in solitary
in the silence of the x-ray room
the waiting and waiting
pondering the unfinished

bullet had my name

spelt wrong

Poem For Eighteen Lost Women

…love is not goodness, and nor it is it happiness…love is the universe touching, exploding within one human being, and that person exploding into the universe. It is annihilation, the destroyer of worlds. – Richard Flanagan, *The Narrow Road To the Deep North*

this is no love poem
but a poem about love

I don't travel well any more
when I stare out of windows
daydreams burn my heart
places and emotions jumble
in a miasma of melancholy
that leaves me unable to breathe

you birthed futures in me
glittering points in the darkness
helped me exhale through racked breath
exorcised the junk of my life
the trivia of so many stupid yesterdays
till my nerves grew to only sense you

never sure who was spreading out most
you-in-me or me-in-you
I felt like a sapling sometimes
growing into your fertile earth
my world full of sky
and gentle rain

I got closer to you
than you were to yourself

now I catch wisps and eddies
glimpses and whispers
your songs echo through this home
catch you in peripheral vision
dancing while you dry your hair
your hands opened out
holding the precious gems
you gave to me

suddenly I breathe the perfume of you
oh yes my skin remembers

The Poet Goes To War

sat in the library in Geelong
every day for a fortnight
took my mind off Hitler
and the certain storm approaching
read Brooke and Owen
poet soldiers in the trenches
at Ypres and Passchendaele
all those shells all that noise
stanzas drenched in mud and blood
never prepared me for this

up the Track at Isurava
plenty of mud and blood for sure
hot humid days and chilling nights
digging in chowing down
gritting teeth clenching rifles
waiting for the Japs again
head on or through the trees
how the hell are there so many?
and we just chocolate soldiers
expected to melt but we haven't

just a green militia battalion
they sent us up to Moresby
told us to pack for a tropical holiday
took my camera and tennis racket
bombed on the airstrip on the second day
we never found Col and only bits of Dennis
now in the forest twilight I am dug in
awaiting the heavy hand of violence
with dysentery and god knows what
and a festering cut on my head

yesterday on the forest floor
our patrol made a dozen contacts
they appeared like ghosts in a green fog
three more of us and maybe ten of them
never leaving this horrid jungle
the Jap I cornered as young as me
lost control of his bowels right there
I flashed on his family back home
how they would take the news
shot him twice in the chest

if the AIF miraculously appear
and me and my mates in the 39th
get out of this dark infested hell
I will forever be fighting in my dreams
like the dangerous ghosts we are now
bright shiny harbingers of death
if I get home alive one day
I will surely write a poem to those
who ran out of luck in Kokoda
those dazzling phantoms of dark misfortune

Ningiwi

early morning…present
up earlier than i want
drained from a dream-laden sleep
grey sky…present
been drizzling through dawn
now the scattering on metal roof
thunderstorm…imminent
a change thumping up from the south
will get my dogs barking most likely
headache…present
my unwanted companion
barometrically induced pain
palm trees…present
greenery surrounding the space
i like the word verdant
water feature…fluidly present
marble dolphins in a synchronised swim
tinkling away twenty-four-seven
planters couch…present
floral cushions in green white and silver
encouraging all manner of lounging
coffee table…solidly present
a whopping piece of red river gum
on squat recycled legs

succulents…doggedly present
like creation had a few drunk years
turning out botanical comedy
incense…nebulously present
sandalwood patchouli and ylang ylang
drifting into my face on changing airs
iPod…present
ryuichi sakamoto's japanese piano
eking out emotion from an antique yamaha
the novel I'm reading set in my birthplace
has many names to keep track of
no tick for that
coffee…present for a while
ground in the garage every morning
east timor fair trade going down nicely
dogs…ever present
hanging on every micro-movement
expecting a beach excursion
house and garden present all round
a place named ningiwi
'i am home' from the ojibwa
laptop…battery forty per cent present
enough to finish this poem
to fix this time and space

Cullens Road Ghost

passed him again yesterday evening
on one of the tighter curves
where the forest leans in dark
drove inside the arc of his orange Datsun
its old motor belching and farting
face taut through his windscreen
just enough of a sighting
to see whitened knuckles on the wheel

a quarter of a century he has tracked
the winding rural forest road
in the frigid dawn air of winter
the silent bush sleeping in late
in the rising heat of summer
bell birds chiming the speeding minutes
of a phantom mired in struggle
escaping the sucking drudgery of his home

twenty-five years up and down that road
doomed to a tight neck and constant frown
if I could flag down his car
the two of us would lean on the bonnet
I'd be beside myself then
I could tell the poor man
I would one day get away
and I would be released

but in this gloomy twilight
under the threatening darkness
he looks so damned haunted
his sadness has me shivering

Bridge Crossing

'We cross our bridges as we come to them and burn them behind us, with nothing to show for our progress except a memory of the smell of smoke, and the presumption that once our eyes watered.' – Tom Stoppard, *Rosencrantz and Guildenstern Are Dead*

most days there
I didn't want to see
what little was left
in the core of me

no need for blood tests
or forensic reports
to know I had bled
among the city's throng

prayed daily for mercy
the gift of amnesia
how could I not
rise up and fly away?

home is that place
where if you must go
they must take you in
but here would do

smoke stench in my hair
wide red eyes watering
but in the flame of today
glows a luminous tomorrow

Daughter of Isfahan

it's come to this then
razor wire and watchtowers
my engineering doctorate pointless
fluent in Farsi French and English
they say I should go back where I came from

descendant of Darius
daughter of Isfahan
student in Tehran
forced into the Iranian diaspora
the guards call me Iraqi bitch

I see my ignorant captors
on their side of the razor wire
numbingly smug in their lucky country
more imprisoned than me
convinced I'm another terrorist

yet we have in common
abhorrence of mass murder
hatred for fundamentalism
and a love of free speech
now used to call me a bloody Arab

quarantined at the end of the world
my family in an ocean graveyard
they go home to their happy families
leaving me to stare at dead banana trees
later to dream of my unlucky country

I Tamas

I was one of many skinny kids
in schools in those times
we still had a ration book
the government keeping tabs
on butter bacon eggs and more
and the money wasn't there
for seconds puddings or sweets

sitting at a desk of my own
maybe I was an odd-one
never occurred at the time
struggling with the three Rs
eyes on Mrs Hart's blackboard
the door opened behind us all
it was the Head and a very wiry kid

the Head in his ill-fitting suit
half encouraged half dragged the waif
to the front next to the dusty easel
he talked with Mrs Hart and left
the boy had big dark-lined eyes
which darted around like prey
on the edge of tears I thought

children this is Tamas
you can call him Tommy
he's from a country called Hungary
they're having some trouble there
so he's come here to school
you will look after him John
come here Tamas sit in this chair

even skinnier than the worst of us
and his jumper was holed and smelly
I got back to my 7 and 9 times tables
he looked at my page took his pencil
and finished the lot before even Nigel
that day we said nothing
later we broke down some walls

he copied my English and got smacked
I copied his arithmetic and got whacked too
the low-achievers liked him
only in arithmetic he beat them
he took the heat off the weird kids as well
but his eyes lit when the football came out
we all wanted 'the magician' in our team

out in the playground it was always
elelmiszer elelmiszer elelmiszer
as he pointed to his mouth
and we did give him food sometimes
half an apple, a piece of white bread or a sweet
he loved it that we had the word 'hungry'
he an insatiable embodiment of it

the boy was living with a vicar's family
never a word to us about his own
when I pushed it with him it was always
tanks boom boom fall down much peoples
I can see him today shouting at our grey skies
it was like a mantra for that month with us
I Tamas I Budapest I Magyar

Bewilderness

the sky bothers me

bewitches with its splendid visions
distracts from my strange and awkward life

how can I worry about diminishing finances
when clouds like granite-coloured cream
come thumping over my home?

fret about work not finished
when a sunset like psychedelic paisley
sends an orange pink glow around the rooms?

get anxious over burgeoning arthritis
when fair weather cumulus skid in azure skies
in air so clear I fear for its oxygen content?

the midnight blue of late twilight's void
and pearlised overcast skies

stop me in my footprints

Green Bikini

submerged under the bay
tapping two rocks
smashing off some shellfish
for the big blue gropers
greedy for free food

holding my breath
air still in the snorkel
vision cut down by my mask
she glided above the rocks
in her green bikini

she swam back past me
beckoned me up to the surface
adjusted her mask
pointed into the water
dived down deep again

swimming like porpoises
twisting around each other
an arcane aquatic ritual
with a woman I didn't know
whose face I had not seen

back on land she stripped
off came the snorkel and mask
held the towel for her
when the bikini came off
pretended not to look

fish salad wine and coffee
lasted all the hot afternoon
as we stripped back our lives
laid bare our hopes and plans
pinched myself under the table

at twilight walked back to my car
damp towel around my neck
flippers and mask in my hand
phone number in my pocket
spring in my step

Escape Act

enough of data entry
into now quaint computers
enough of selling books on the Third Reich
to hassled housewives in Pennant Hills
enough of the car wash
accused of nicking ashtray change
I ring the number put aside for a month
when can you start?

we need a science teacher
who can teach English to refugees
what the heck for?
the English of science you serious?
atomic structure to Cambodians
classification of organisms to Afghans
evolution to Vietnamese
energy and motion to Iranians?

Dith and his lost sister
a whole family wiped by Pol Pot
I show *The Killing Fields* to the class
he claims it a comedy in comparison
Thi Kim who never stops smiling
like she's still in Saigon and the war never came
puts her arm round the new ones from everywhere
eases them gently into Sydney

Saman who's father's rug shop in Tehran's best street
is ransacked by Khomeini's goons
they confiscate rugs beat up his mother
waits to grow up and vent his rage back there
Johnny who lost his family in a Beirut fire fight
hides out for three years in the Shouf Mountains
fronts up smiling every day and helps us with the chores
the Red Cross find his family intact and on their way

Abdul who insists on a prayer room
gets into a scrape with a Tongan giant
who wants to beat him up
until he hears he's killed four Russians
Shoaib who's going to be late so I pick him up in my car
hot morning short sleeves and I see hundreds of scars
Mujahideen? I say before I've thought it out
No sir! Tandoori oven

I marvel at taps clean water hot water showers
fresh food on my table from the whole world
but at night I dream their dreams
their impossible dreams of sleep with no gunfire
then I'm back in front of my class
an escapee from Thatcher's Britain
in front of these real refugees
better act like I understand

High Time

rarely searching mountain tops or walking at heights of eagles
just busy having a high old time
usually just free-falling into accidental futures
living with the dispassion of too many years in one place

always one eye on the slipping of time
the other scanning the horizon
was high time a high tide brought my future to me
and let it lap around my aching feet

there is no light on anyone that casts no shadows
but you rose like another sun over the landscapes of me
you set me spinning so I had no dark side at all
your trajectory across my sky was a slow singing arc

your voice echoing off the walls
whispered of swirling mist but shouted of sub-tropical surf
and I could only feel my future falling
heavily around me like hot sweating nights

lightning played exquisite havoc with my nervous system
leaves on the jacaranda outside your room submitted to gravity
and a million miraculous truths lay deep around our daytime hours
too deeply cut inside to ever let go

I Love You Afghans…

…even your graffiti artists
spray Rumi on your walls

east along the Welayat Road to the Aqaha Mosque
the taxi driver stares with hawkish eyes
in a rear vision mirror hung with lapis beads
screws his eyes up and hums
I ask how far
when the moon is troubled
it is not from its view of the sun
but the radiance of the friend
be drunken with that light
or pass your cup to me

next morning passing tied up camels and donkeys
I hit the market in Baghcheh-E-Metar
smell of tea and bread ovens
attempt to buy dates and pomegranates
how much?
my jailed heart has escaped
running up mountains
speak not of tomorrow
or days incarcerated
only of now in your sunlight left to dance

outside the tomb of Molana Vaeez Keshevi that evening
he thumps the sand and dust off a rich red carpet
shouts at the kids to get away from the stall
settles down on a chair next to his dog
can I look at the carpet you just beat?
wake now the beloved is in your room
don't choose to stay there
elope and hide in mountain caves
run down and drink clear stream water
when all is dark as grace

*In Herat you couldn't stretch a leg out
without poking a poet up the arse…*

'I love you Afghans – even your graffiti artists spray Rumi on your walls.' from *And the Mountains Echoed* by Khaled Hosseini; 'In Herat you couldn't stretch a leg out without poking a poet up the arse.' from *A Thousand Splendid Suns* by Khaled Hosseini, both published by Bloomsbury Press

Pluviophile

i enjoy a solar massage
the warm sun on my back
unravelling the myofibres
between the blades

then the deluge for days on end
weeks of splashing torrents
and i get surprised by the solace
found in showers and pouring rainstorms

smiling at a vanished horizon
across concrete coloured water
with dripping hair and sodden shoes
a bedraggled dog by my side

in this country of gorgeous heat
dare I come out
admit what I've become?
a lover of rain

OK Commuter

so cold so dark so early
wind off the water lets you know
you underdressed again

hot coffee with sugar cupped in two hands
your neck muscles tensed under your scarf
on the business-grey platform

you yawn and shut your eyes to it all
palms reefs and warm lapping water
dreams of searing hot days

which are no better than this
when you must be on a train anyway
five days in five days out

week upon week month after month
yearning like a homesick migrant
for just an imminent public holiday

you pray to the god of small things
that she will be on
doing her make-up like she's in your bedroom

you pray to the deity of the miniscule
that he will not be on
droning on and no word edgeways for his girl

the next train on platform one
will eat seventy-five minutes of your life
hold you a frozen captive

force you to your ipod playlists
cause you to text when you can get a signal
make you finish the stupid spy story

force you to ponder words like routine
cause you to worry that the rat race
can only be won by rats

the doors swish aside
the wordless regulars in their regular seats
OK commuter grit those teeth

Gerald's Shout

there were trolls in the tunnel
according to Gerald's older brother
and we were every one of us convinced
none of us brave enough to test it

the stream gurgled through the trolls' lair
in winter we crossed above it on the road
through biting cold wind and sleet
the odd strange noise quickening our step

the stream tinkled all summer too
as we played pirates cowboys and soldiers
on the grassy verges and road nearby
running off at any sudden weird boom

we made boats of leaves and sticks
floated them in upstream
ran across the ten-yard road
they never came out the other side

we didn't dare ask any grown ups
scared enough by the prospect of ridicule
at eight years old you have a lot of secrets
shared only with your friends

we told the girls about it of course
elaborated and exaggerated
frightened them with hideous descriptions
said we'd seen their faces in the tunnel's mouth

Gerald and Steven and me in spring
up the inside of the hollow tree
pulled a wasp nest down on us
and fell in a tangle to the ground

the wasps attacked us like demons
our arms flailed about
we panicked and ran pursued
headlong towards the stream

Steven's shout, jump in the water!
all three of us fell in splashing crazily
right through the trolls' supposed den
out the other side laughing with relief

wiped the smiles when we saw the girls
Gerald's shout: the trolls have wasps!
the trolls have wasps!
they scampered screaming

we fell about crying with laughter
Gerald plotted revenge on his brother
Steven sang I'm a troll fol-de-rol
while he wrung out his shirt

the myth now blown apart
we had a new place to play
I wiped the snot off my lip
my fat wasp-stung lip

Jungle

she came by yesterday
all swagger and twitch
robust little girl
how dare she think!

early hot sunrise
six of our girls
waiting on the wall
ambush mode

sometimes the girls
let us go along too
observer role only
boys out of their depth

we have to stay back
not get in the way
while girls do their work
furious fatal work

came by again today
swaggering twitching
strong-looking girl
attractive in a way

two girls drop over the edge
their mouths grab her flank
she sheds her waggling tail
others will pick that up later

two more jump down
now it's easy to drag her
up the wall over the back
she will never go home

we are all plain skinks
she was yellow-striped
our girls keep the clan pure
they will eat her best parts

Granite

always had an array of red-themed shirts
couple of pairs of black jeans
my early morning default clothing
these days greys and silvers get intrusive
echoing the process going on with my hair
but I've worn the whole lot at some time
an extensive range of stylish colours

always been able to lie and bake in the sun
watch the motes and glints play in my eyes
wounds healed fast with no hint of tetanus
all right there are scars all over me
you could shine some as yet unknown light
and highlight invisible marks on my skin
not quite heat scratch and stain resistant

pruning weeding repotting
green fingers right up to my shoulders
can drill hammer fix minor things
can cook a curry fix a good coffee
can wash and sew
drive like the best
maintenance free

got through my childhood alive
no small feat there
and the collateral damage
rearing up later on
got held to the light
smashed apart and sorted
durable and functional it turns out

three bike crashes that should have broken me
a car crash that could have caved my skull
43 years of football survived
impact resistant me

wash my hands like granny told me
extremely hygienic

in dreams both day and night
get glimpses of the substance I am
the basic material I'm made of
intrusive felsive igneous
phaneritic porphyritic
crystalline

tough

Mango

the seed a storage silo of nutrients
ready to drill down into ground
preparing to launch at the sky
just add spring rain

spindly sapling rushing skyward
sprouting at angles prompted by DNA
and the track of the seasonal suns
adolescent hanging out by the shed

mango tree very pretty
long fingered leaves of dusky green
smooth bark twisting at the sun
botanical sculpture in the garden

tiny green and cream florets
look like nothing much
get knocked off in a stiff breeze
but they have the scent of the fruit

when you're slopping mango juice
down your wrists in a humid 33
it's a sneak preview of heaven
then you floss orange fibres from your teeth

University of Pluto Inner Solar System Field Trip 2286 Travel Advice

Venus

stay inside the station
it's acid rain out there
the longest day in the whole system
will feel like a day at uni to you
hot rocky and volcanic
rent a sulphuric acid suit
go on the Venusian Volcano Tour
3 stars

Mercury

one side faces the sun
gets hot as hell
the other will freeze a limb off
in under ten seconds
go on the border walk
zig zag across from -170 to +420
in a complimentary thermo-suit
a day is longer than a year
breakfast in spring
lunch in summer
you get the drift
2 stars

Mars

*Mars ain't the kind of place
to raise your kids* – Elton John
but it is the place for jewellery
take home an iron oxide bangle
rust never looked so good
see both moons
from the viewing dome
eat dinner in the Martian Bar
ancient Mars-related movies
on a constant loop
4 stars

Earth

all you can do there now
is visit the Global Warming Museum
worth a stopover
see where we came from
1 star

Let Himself Go

his note exploded into a thousand shards
put an end to her recent purple patch
her future now dead as cold stone

he'd left the house frigid and quiet
never again to carry her excess baggage
lug around her invisible neuroses

surrounded by his rejected paraphernalia
wringing her hands in front of the mirror
her sobbing ruptured the silence

she wanted to step off a cliff and let salt waves close over
a potential aneurysm thought better of it and backed off
nerves snapped their wiring

she'd said he wasn't the man he was
she'd said he'd let himself go
and so he did

Nemophilist

I know I would be haunted
by visions of dark forests
of ironbarks and blackbutt trees
straggling over sandstone
running down steep hillsides
in full view of the Pacific
at their edges different trees
she-oaks that sough like voices
in autumn southerly winds
invasive lantana bushes
with their pungent flowers
and in the sudden clearings
black-boys with spears
that I try to call xanthorrhoea
the sudden flash of glary sun rays
on the smooth salmon pinks
of the rubber-looking red gums
cockatoos gaggling in the crowns
the screech of lorikeets in the spaces
crazy formation stunt flyers
and the watching tawny frogmouth
you must be silent and still to see
and only if luck is with you anyway
drop low and see the micro world
a thousand species of moss
huntsman spiders and blue centipedes
bull ants that can spice up your walk
skinks dropping over logs
a goanna shinning up the tree
takes your eye to a green tree snake

reminding you that this is reptile country
the indrawn breaths of eucalyptus
hit you in your own reptilian brain
if I ever left the Great South Land
I know I would be haunted

Anjing

the *anjing* had followed me for half an hour
her head down and her eyes wide and haunted
I walked she limped along the grid of narrow paths
marking out the rice fields of Ubud
the hot space ringed by palms and papaya trees

you are the one

rice workers greeted me with their *selamat siangs*
greeted the *anjing* with shouts and raised sticks
and a respectful sneering caution
but she never took her focus from me
limping on you'd have to say doggedly

take me to your home

we passed a losman garden with guests drinking tea
they shouted there's a dog following me
they say she's got rabies
I say she's hungry
but she doesn't touch the offerings outside

let me share your food

we came onto the Monkey Forest Road
but not one monkey breaks cover today
yesterday an ambush and stolen fruit
they jibbered and chattered in the trees instead

wary of *anjing* teeth
I will watch your back

in the main street lined with *warungs*
you can get food and carved wooden trinkets
and everything from tea strainers to brassieres
they shouted in Bahasa Indonesia
get rid of that *anjing* following you

you are my leader

dog no good give her kick she go
gado gado and *kachang hijau* please
and a large chicken with rice
a man aimed his arm at the *anjing*
she flinched but held her ground

I am your dog now

I crouched low tapped my leg
come here girl
she limped forward panting in the white heat
her head low big brown eyes looking up
nuzzled my leg

I crave your affection

we walked down to the lotus pond
she comes up softly in front of me
here girl chicken is all I can do for you
wish I could take you home with me
selamat tinggal anjing girl

I would take a bullet for you

Good God

'will make thee in Mine Own image'
more of a mirror image really
write My name down
now reflect it – see?
(partial to oblique humour)

going to be a shock for you
when you go to your heaven
find it's called rainbow bridge
and you're outnumbered
by the whole canine gamut

while you're still down on earth
be happy be ecstatic even
dogs are My way
of apologising
for your relatives

Ogre

'Yet she did remember him saying in a quiet reflective voice something about 'those of us who are bound to submit our bodies to the ogres', and the thought penetrated her marrow as a reference to the sort of life she was leading.' – Lawrence Durrell, *The Alexandria Quartet*

in hushed revelations with friends
it got very prepositional
first he had got near then come close
heavy-set and brutish-looking
she felt fascinated and repelled
but beside him next day anyway
alongside the oversized hominid

they could all see the grotesque quite clearly
though she was struck deaf and blind
not for the first time around an oversized hulk
knowing deep inside he would tear her flesh away
cannibalise her thoughts her ideas and reason
distant from her used-up body in no time

she was oblivious to both the odour of him
and her own stench of burning martyr
coupling with another incarnation of Grendel*
while she felt it was a cute Shrek** she kissed
in yet another chapter of gullible's travails...

* Grendel: the ogre in Beowulf, the Anglo-Saxon epic poem
** Shrek: the ogre in the recent animated film of the same name

Strangely Strange But Oddly Normal

stoats ferrets voles and badgers
were supposed to be around
but I never clapped eyes on one
a fox for sure killed one of our hens
and I did see one on a hillside once
red red robins never did much bobbing
anywhere I ever lived
had to settle for Christmas card pics
starlings and sparrows were what you got

through customs to get Downunder
welcome to *Terra Australis*
welcome to the Great South Land
remnant of Gondwana
welcome to The Zoo

yep I've seen the snakes
my Oz-born girlfriend back then
trod on one by our tent
we packed the gear up and left
jumped out of the car for a pee last year
and surprised a red-bellied black
no jokes please
I've done them all
so has every other bugger
a young brown snake was spotted
in the front garden just once
skinks scatter wherever I walk now
the dogs keep the blue-tongues away
or I'd be stumbling over them for sure
have cohabited with goannas in forests
fed them by hand with fish and eggs
fed them by leaving the esky unguarded

that really is weird…

and the spiders abound
spiders that jump I was told
caught plenty of funnel webs
and sent them for milking
more than once while tidying up
shredded bark and twigs after storms
I have grabbed by mistake
a shocked katydid and recoiled
did I mention the mozzies?
big bastards that carry you to bed

if you're thinking of staying up
huntsmen are allowed in the bathroom
to get the big-bastard mozzies
kept a pet cockroach early on
even gave him an alliterative name
Conrad needed to stay in the kitchen
he didn't and was evicted without fuss

you're joking that makes no sense…

things in the ocean they said
which can kill you so fast
you won't even get out
done my share of surfing and swimming
not a single sighting of a shark
no cause for alarm there then
though was gaped at and lunged at
by a whopping great wobbegong
five metres under snorkeling down south

and that is what pray tell?

it's the birds the cackling birds
the laughing birds the warbling birds
the squeaking screeching bird life
the whipbirds and bellbirds
the birds in coats of many colours
the magpies which seem to like me
Margaret and Maurice that patrol out the front
come hopping over for leftover dog food
and the pee-wees that attacked me

when we first moved in on their patch
no one at customs prepared me for them

what the heck is that?

nothing weird to me now
all common as red dirt
but every night it sits up there
in the enormous white-trunked gum
high up on the same branch in the dark
a thing from another time and place

a green fluorescent glow…

Five Patonga Haiku

Wild blooms stretch skyward.
Over the bay above the flowers
the whistling kite careens.

From a cloudy sky
a pelican diverts its flightpath,
checks out the black dog.

Dawn spills on the land.
Sleepy fishermen catch sluggish fish.
It's another hot one!

Daisies and zinnias
jostle sharp succulents in the dunes.
Fire threatens over hills…

The southerly blows,
conquers sand surf and plants, but never
fifteen regal pines.

Trust

right in front of him right now
the loyal river gliding green
transporting its aquatic cargo
of algae and weeds
sticks and driftwood out of the forest
a hundred metres past him
into a cacophony downstream
a cascade of boiling devils
a cataract of hellish foam

cross-legged and back-arched
sipping a last coffee
from a chipped enamel cup
taste and smell now heightened
to those of a bloodhound

it had been rolling in for years
settling as sediments
quanta pressing down on quanta

they had let him down
disdainfully with clumsy abandon
then with a violent thud

he had thought to get through
but any notion of touch-wood
had long departed his hopes
to be replaced by wallow-in-sawdust

then this then bloody this
the words straw and last had surfaced

now he implored his loyal river
to let him down gently

Fifty Years

'I don't know how you've put up with him all these years, Vera. He's very difficult.'
'Worse than that. He's a self-centred grumpy bastard with no empathy for anyone else. He's expecting to be celebrating fifty years of marriage next July. He's in for a shock…'
'What?'

if there was a final straw
it was the tea towel

Rio de Janeiro
my flight is booked
it's one way
day before our 50th
golden wedding anniversary
ha ha what gold?
if I were back in '65
with Alf approaching
wearing his gormless grin
going down on his knees
popping the proverbial
the answer would be no
go away bugger off
the next 50 years of my life
are not going to be wrecked
ruined and generally stuffed
by an annoying git like you
go and find some horrid woman
who deserves a horrid man
what the hell was I thinking?

we're going out
I put on stilettos
a beautiful red dress
make him proud
he comes in from the garage
grubby sport shoes
old stonewash jeans
and that stupid bloody rugby shirt
jangles the car keys
dirt under his nails
still that gormless grin

his sister gave us the tea towel
it was like a cotton photo of me
the lady beautifully clothed
wearing her kitchen pinafore
looking vacant yet distressed
poised to jump off the jetty
let the water wash over her

the day he had expected to celebrate
fifty years of holy wedlock
he'll be down the RSL instead
drowning his sorrows
and I'll be on Ipanema Beach
feeling the warm sunny glow

oh I'll jump all right
in my bikini
let the water wash
through nearly fifty years
of unholy deadlock

Enter Stage Left

took my seat on the train to Gloucester Central
cold compartment after freezing platform
at Birmingham New Street station
burrowed down in my old trench coat
then in walked Michael York

sat opposite in his expensive gabardine mac
complained about the cold and buffet food
asked where I was going to
he was going to Cheltenham Spa
to visit his aunt

wanted to ask him about *Romeo and Juliet*
his Tybalt in Zeffirelli's film adaptation
but decided not to let on I knew him
instead we talked about university
he'd graduated from Oxford in '64

he asked what subject I was studying
(enter stage left a trainee maths teacher)
actually I'm studying astrophysics
then for nearly forty minutes
I played opposite Michael York

Snakes and Ladders

king cobra in my cot at 1
killed with a machete
at 2 under the waves
hat bobbing on the sea
crashed my bike at 14
rescued by the truck driver
at 16 the electric shock
unconscious and connected to the mains
avoided fatal car crash at 22
overslept while my friends died
at 26 the rooftop accident
saved by flimsy guttering

each near miss 50 50
odds are even
half a chance
you climb up the ladder
half a chance
you slither down the longest snake
stop dead right there
the debates about cremation
the search for nice things to say
you end up under a flowering gum

I'm no more than 1 in 64
yet somehow 100% here

The Lamentation of Bobby the Airedale

that was some find!

hardwood sticks my favourites
with shreds of hanging bark
dropped from the tree in my garden
crunched on those all day

soft flexible ones too
had their qualities
they twanged if I did it wrong
flicked me in the face

then the ones with twigs on
their leaves made a puzzle of it
stripped the whole lot off
and ripped them right up

driftwood like wooden bones
tasted of salt like the ocean
those were like a challenge in stone
never got enough time for them

would chase after any stick
chucked in the park by the boss
he could fling them quite far off
always carried them back well balanced

but some find that one was!
smooth and gleaming
brown and bending
then it slipped under a log

the terrier in me surfaced
landed me in the vet's
in pain and shutting down
how was I to knew it could bite?

a transfusion from a mastiff
gave me just one more year
I chased a few chewed a few
then this nothing

The Fridge Magnet Poems

SING LIKE NO ONE CAN HEAR YOU
tried that
I didn't want to hear me
BE THE KIND OF PERSON YOUR DOG THINKS YOU ARE
trying to avoid being that
an idiot human who can't lead or communicate in canine
LOVE IS A FRIENDSHIP SET ON FIRE
sometimes we get on
like a house under water
FOLLOW YOUR BLISS
done my duty is all
bliss hasn't entered into it more than transiently
DARE TO BE REMARKABLE
now that is funny
I don't dare to even be mediocre
I'M NOT A COMPLETE IDIOT
SOME PARTS OF ME ARE MISSING
let me count these parts
honesty integrity bravery
are the least of them
MY MIND NOT ONLY WANDERS
IT SOMETIMES LEAVES COMPLETELY
just reconnoitering for the day
when it won't have to return

Shipwreck

some days I wade out
past the slosh of the bubbling surf
into salty turquoise tepid reaches
don the weighty brass helmet
dive deep deep deep
into a world where wrecks
sunk in forgotten battles
creak through the brine
75 years of grinding rusting dissolving
has rendered them into reefs
now homes and proving grounds
for hundreds of coloured fish
drift past the skeletons
of sailors from those battles
tougher men than me
still I head down
plunge into the weirdest fathoms
where the eccentric sea life hangs out
till my eardrums must shred

standing on the seabed today
something is quite right

through swirls of eddying deep greens
materialising through sandy wisps
the reason today's dive
will become a salvage mission

my refurbished gleaming metal hulk
ready to be floated to the surface

The Previous Panic of Robert Stamford

there
there had to be
there had to be a word
there had to be a word for the feeling
there had to be a word for the feeling that he was going
there had to be a word for the feeling that he was going suddenly
there had to be a word for the feeling that he was going suddenly
to kiss her

walk at a normal pace
take care not to be distracted
by orange and crimson resin
leaking from gum trees
secretive flowers peering from tiny crevices
walk for just over six minutes
see a pink red gum branch
duck under and turn left
take about fifteen steps
there are four ironbarks
go behind them you will see

written 35 years back
on his only other trip to this promontory
between two wondrous beaches

RS heart JT

there she is again laughing
turning on her heel

like back then

CPSIA information can be obtained
at www.ICGtesting.com
Printed in the USA
LVHW011640260819
628959LV00014B/1236